AGAINST ROMANCE

POEMS BY

MICHAEL BLUMENTHAL

Pleasure Boat Studio: A Literary Press
New York

AGAINST ROMANCE
By Michael Blumenthal

Copyright 2006

Library of Congress Cataloging-in-Publication
Data:

Blumenthal, Michael.
    Against Romance: poems / by Michael Blumenthal
        p. cm.
        ISBN: 9781-929355-23-8 (alk.paper)
            I. Title.

PS3552.L849A7 2005
811'.54-dc22

First published in 1987 by Viking Penguin Inc.

Published by Pleasure Boat Studio: A Literary Press
201 West 89th Street
New York, NY 10024
Tel/Fax: 888-810-5308
e-mail: pleasboat@nyc.rr.com
www.pleasureboatstudio.com

for Howard Nemerov

The things that flew and the things that fell,
The heartbreaks and the triumphs on the page,
The sprinkler down so low it couldn't tell
Humility from pride, or love from rage.

These all comprise the homages of man,
Of man to man, of woman, stone and child,
Of spirit fiddlings papered down in pen
By these once-lustful bards now grown so mild.

So goes this anti-romance, now, into the air,
Inscribed to one who drove me to this gaming
Yet warned me, by his blessing, to beware—
For you, dear friend, so aptly named for naming.

Mon Dieu, hear the poet's prayer.
The romantic should be here.
The romantic should be there.
It ought to be everywhere.
But the romantic must never remain . . .

—WALLACE STEVENS, "Sailing after Lunch"

He loved. He loves. And will love.
But he doesn't want his love
to be a prison for two,
a contract between yawns,
and four feet in bedroom slippers.
Passionate at first meeting,
dry, the second time,
agreeable, the third,
one might say he's afraid
of being fatally human.

—CARLOS DRUMMOND DE ANDRADE, "The Table"
(Elizabeth Bishop, translator)

"Observe, then, that you do not consider Love to be a God."—
"What then," I said, "is Love a mortal?"—"By no means."—
"But what, then?"—"Like those things which I have in-
stanced, he is neither mortal nor immortal, but something
intermediate."—"What is that, O Diotima?"—"A great
Daemon, Socrates; and everything daemoniacal holds an
intermediate place between what is divine and what is mortal."

—PLATO, "The Symposium"

CONTENTS

I. AGAINST ROMANCE

It Happens   3

The Dangers of Metaphor   5

Mt. Auburn Cemetery   6

The Romanticist   7

The Foreshadowings   8

The Chambermaid   9

Separated   10

Museum Piece   12

Overwhelming   13

Separate Rooms   14

A Modern Alphabet   15

A Marriage   16

At Lucy Vincent Beach,
Easter Sunday, 1986   17

Against Romance   18

For/Against   20

Death of a Romantic   22

II. CIVILITIES

Good Intentions   25

Manners   26

What a Time!   27

Garments   29

Academic Suppers   30

Charm   *31*

To Each His Own   *32*

Civilities   *34*

The Artichokes of Midnight   *35*

L'Addition   *37*

For a Friend, Having Abandoned All He
Once Stood For   *38*

Renovations   *39*

Suburban   *40*

The Letting   *41*

III. THE ART OF POETRY

The Tip of the Iceberg   *45*

The Word *Love*   *46*

Trying to Learn Basketball at 37   *47*

Seven O'Clock Muse   *49*

Stamps   *50*

A Modern Poet   *51*

The Pleasures of Abstraction   *52*

Advice to My Students: How
to Write a Poem   *54*

Dancing with a De-constructionist   *55*

Prayer to Be Recited after a
Jacques Derrida Lecture   *56*

It Is Best Not to Sit at Your
Desk Too Long, but to Rise   57

The New Yorker Poem   59

Brevities   60

The Source   63

IV. THE HEARTS OF MEN

The Walkers of Hurricanes   67

A Man Grieves Always for the Ships He Has
Missed   68

Skototropic   70

Dr. Wuschti   71

Lucky   72

The Happy Nihilist   73

The Hearts of Men   74

Etymology Lesson on the Road to Rome   76

The Heart of Quang Duc   77

The Man Who Needed No One   79

The Scullers   80

Trip to Bountiful   81

The New Story of Your Life   83

V. STILLNESSES

The Mountains of Evening   87

The Lovers Sleep Late on Sunday.
It Is Good.   89

Grace   90

The Analysand   92

Somewhere Else   95

Stones in Love   96

Winter Solstice, 1983   97

Before Bonnard's *The Terrace*,
Sunday Afternoon   98

Patience   99

The Beautiful Is the Familiar   100

The Pleasures of Old Age   101

Doubled   102

Halved   103

Dusk: Mallards on the Charles River   104

The End   105

Author's Note   107

▲▲ I ▲▲

AGAINST ROMANCE

The poor fellow. He had just begun to suffer from it, this miserable trick the romantic plays upon himself: of setting just beyond his reach the very thing he prizes.

—WALKER PERCY, *The Moviegoer*

It Happens

A man wakes. A woman wakes.
In the separate countries
that are their bodies, it is always
a season, a time of some fruitfulness,
and in their eyes they reveal
the shaken fruition of separate light,
the auspices of an empire
entirely their own. There are flowers
in the vase, tulips perhaps,
and, outside, small flakes of snow
feathering into the streets
are a sign of some seasonal ascendancy,
a grief too separate from them
to be of interest, yet part
of the world's wild order, part
of the making that will become them.

All night, they have shaken their wishes
from themselves like sequins, and they
reach out now, from the rapt attentiveness
of their bodies, to find each other again
in the semi-shock of a world peopled and disparate,
remote yet touchable. He, perhaps, has dreamt
of deer in a yard somewhere, goats
rubbing their clipped horns against a fence,
while she, she is thinking, as he reaches out
to place a hand on her beautiful thigh,
of the red carnation some man once gave her,
in a crowded station in some country
she no longer remembers. The white light
of a wintry day enters the room, and they
do not yet know how great, or small, will be

their love for one another, they do not yet know
whether the song they had sung last night '
will survive the resurrected pasts of separate sleep,
whether the whiteness of this dawn is the white
of a clean slate, or merely a fog night has issued
over a continuing clarity, whether love
is really love at all, or whether
what happened before has happened again
and they are two separate empires once more—
drifting off and drifting on, reaching out
for what they once thought was dry land
but is only, alas, another profundity
of deep waters and strange occupants, things
too far beneath the surface to reach out and touch,
to see or to feel, too deep
for even flesh to answer to, or to call.

The Dangers of Metaphor

Metaphors are not to be trifled with. A single metaphor can give birth to love.

—Milan Kundera

The day when the rainbows came,
I was running up a steep hill toward you,
and, looking up to find you there, said:
That rainbow looks like a halo
around your head. These
were my first words to you
and, ever since, I have held you
against the sky, the way a man holds
a closed letter to the light without opening it,
and what I have seen there is something
I might want to open, carefully,
as if it were addressed to me. But
there are dangers in this, this beginning
with something as heavenly
as a rainbow. So I wait,
holding you up again each day
against a bleaker sky
and you become, this way,
less transparent, less embellished
by the numinous, but more real.
Last night there were no stars anywhere
and, today, desire's prism
held against the sky
yields only a pure white. In fact,
each day now the sky falls
a bit closer to you, merciful
as a guillotine,
keeping you earthbound, flawed—
a human thing only another human thing could love.

Mt. Auburn Cemetery

There are places in the world you associate with loss
and, this being so, you should not go to them,
since the mind will always dollop backward

To its place of pain, since it will gladly generalize
from some happy present to a miserable walk
you once took there with someone, who finally

Abandoned you. So what if the Blackburnian warbler,
with its orange throat, will pass here en route
to some bucolic Virginia? So what if the rufous-

Sided towhee will rummage like a bag lady
among last year's leaves? Darling, I say it
in earnest: *we will never come here,*

We will never traipse among the gravestones
and the beneficent shrubs, we will never picnic
beneath some labeled beech, among the Astors,

Dunns, Beaufords and Gilligans who have been laid
to rest here. No, we will find a place of
our own, we will have to discover some divot

Of earth from which our own failings can rise up
to haunt us. It is this way for everyone:
nothing pristine forever, nothing inviolable.

Surely the good grass and the birds will find us,
entwined in some other shrubbery. And the dead,
believe you me, will take care of their own.

The Chambermaid

Each day she comes into the vacant rooms
to make the beds, those unkempt sheets
where some have loved, and some
have dreamt of love, alone, in sweet
and private dreams. Each day she comes
when those who've slept are gone, her broom

contending with the stained and crumpled floor.
Each day she screens the lusty, turgid air
of sleep, she folds the scattered gowns,
the terminating towels, the seamy underwear
of love, collects the vagrant bits of down
that pillows cough into the night. And shuts the door.

Sometimes she stops to hear the singing of the wren
between her rounds of those who weave their threads
into the tattered blanket of the night, who spin
their yarns in unmade, transitory beds.
And then she's gone, and those newly arrived come in—
to whom love came, and wants to come again.

Separated

The day slants
toward the light it is about to become
and, deep from your borrowed bed,
you rise, alone again
as in your happiest hours,
and you wonder, as you ease yourself
toward the lit corner of the room
where dawn first claims the house,
why, and for what, a man or woman
would barter these first, uninhabited hours
in which the mind moves
like a freshly lit candle
from the near-death of sleep
into the first, warm syllables
of its own creation, in which time moves
like a concertina through its three-tiered scales
and the day becomes, as it should be,
the slow unwinding of the self's discourse
with the self. Fresh from your solipsistic sleep,
you are what you are again: the slim feather
of your own life, a swelled paragraph
in your own book, and you wonder why
a vague guilt drifts into the unshared hours,
why the relinquished bliss passes,
in the secular world, for a kind of nobility,
because today, above all else, you feel
noble once more, like a priest too long banished
from his church, like an exiled king
returning to his kingdom, and you ponder,
in the baptismal light, what guilt,
what sense of unentitlement to your own plenitude,
had brought you there, into the divisive symmetry

of the conjugal bed, and you repeat to yourself
what you have always known courage to be—
the hard resilience to say: *I did, I was,*
I said, I am, the claimed and peculiar light
of your own strange shining. Risen perfectly now
into the shape of your hard-won selfhood,
you sit at the window watching the bricks
become the building and the leaves the trees,
the day relinquish itself to the human world,
which you, praise God, feel part of
once more—but never again too much,
never again like that.

Museum Piece

A man says to his wife, on the subject
of Monet's *La Rue Montorgueil: too
much red*. And she replies: *that's
just what I like about it!* And so another
Sunday afternoon of love among the art lovers:
He pure Baroque, she High Renaissance,
all things a matter of taste—a café au lait
and an artichoke vinaigrette, later that afternoon,
in a small bistro along the avenue, each
now thinking whom else he might have loved,
their Dark Age just around the corner:
already framed and agreed upon in earnest.

Overwhelming

If love is an overwhelming thing
and, wanting it, you are sometimes yourself
overwhelming—that is, you roll over
something, or someone, with the sheer weight
of what you want; if you are this way at times
with the wish to rectify your life,
to make a mid-course correction
because it has overwhelmed you,
and you are out, now, in mad pursuit
of an equilibrium, a coming together
that would be slow, yet overwhelming;
if you have arrived, now,
at the overwhelming conclusion
that love heals almost anything
(though never everything), then
you will deserve to be forgiven
for your haste, you will deserve
to be reprimanded, even slowed,
in your mad pursuit of what is beautiful
and necessary, to be reminded,
perhaps over quail in a Portuguese restaurant,
that love, however urgent, is always slow,
that you've no right to overwhelm
what has overwhelmed you (overwhelming
as it may seem), but you must proceed
as if the things that happened
had never happened, as if by the mere
certainty of your pursuit you could tame
what is overwhelming in yourself—
an excess of enthusiasm for what was missing,
a lack brought quietly home again and made whole.

Separate Rooms

All tenderness, we go our way—
you to your bed, I to mine.
The river runs through the trees,
a plethora of diamonds. The stars
summon their quorums, petitioning
their own stars. The finches and starlings
spread clean sheets over their beds
exchanging lullabies.

This afternoon, we sat on the porch,
lustless and content as octogenarians,
twin closets opening toward each other
into a large room. And now, night folds
its hands over this house, the embers
glowing their final Amens from the fire.

And we close our two-bodied eyes
to dream of another life, far
from desire. From our separate beds.
In these separate rooms, through which
not even our bodies can break
to strangle the river.

A Modern Alphabet

A's wife's in love with B's husband
And see how the delights of their
Easy love are, just like the F-stops
On a *Photoapparat*. All they do is turn
And, gee-whiz, a new view of the world—
Hell with a capital H, so starry-eyed
Has their gleam gone now, as if a
Warbler'd been mistaken for a jay.
KO'd by their lusts, they've made
The elevated rhetoric of love their
Emblem now, and, enticed by the future,
They're open to all suggestions: peaked
Is the once-flat world in their eyes.
Sad ones, they have taken their cues
From their times, and not their gods,
So they are what they are: estuaries
Of less in the name of more. What
A happy tedium they once had, they
Know now: filled with the mortal you
Of the same someone. *Vee haf mounted
To new heights,* her bald German lover
Assures her with his euphemistic view
Of the world. Both their exes are
Sad now, yes, but real and earthbound.
Why, they wonder, is mere contentment
Never enough for some, who, having
A penchant for true bliss, must constantly
Reinvent the alphabet, but always
With the same old story: sad, unwise,
Complete, from A to Z.

A Marriage

for Margie Smigel and Jon Dopkeen

You are holding up a ceiling
with both arms. It is very heavy,
but you must hold it up, or else
it will fall down on you. Your arms
are tired, terribly tired,
and, as the day goes on, it feels
as if either your arms or the ceiling
will soon collapse.

But then,
unexpectedly,
something wonderful happens:
Someone,
a man or a woman,
walks into the room
and holds their arms up
to the ceiling beside you.

So you finally get
to take down your arms.
You feel the relief of respite,
the blood flowing back
to your fingers and arms.
And when your partner's arms tire,
you hold up your own
to relieve him again.

And it can go on like this
for many years
without the house falling.

At Lucy Vincent Beach, Easter Sunday, 1986

Martha's Vineyard

In that long moment when you are trying to decide
whether to kiss someone for the first time
and they are trying to decide whether to kiss you,
the waves break against the rocks
and light shimmies like a skater over the beach,
and you reflect (as her body edges
toward the side of you and she grows—
as men and women will in the dappled light—
increasingly beautiful) on the seeming innocence
of the first kiss, on how, in hundreds
of previous incarnations, you had intended
no evil, but had merely grown,
like a distended flower in early spring,
into the good natural upwardness of all longing,
yes, you reflect on this now, as the gulls waft
like serenity over the waves,
as some larger fidelity patrols the beach
and you realize how meaning follows gesture
into the night, how there is no hurry in this life
aside from death, how today's light will be
resurrected again in tomorrow's dawn, and all
that the tide brings in from the ambiguous sea
will be there for you again, without haste, on some
lovelier tomorrow, and whatever the trembling lips
need to speak, they will ultimately speak, against
whatever the tide brings, whatever it takes away.

Against Romance

The two lovers tangled in the thicket
of their terrible passion do not yet know
one another, but they are delighted,
nonetheless, to be here, on this spring day,
among the periwinkles and crocuses,
because it is part of their beautiful image
of what love is, because they have been
to the cinema and can imagine, now,
a Mozart concerto or a Chopin nocturne
playing in the background, they can imagine
they are like the lovers in Bonnard's *Terrace*,
but supine beneath the horse chestnuts
and magnolias, and that it is all part
of love's wild and ancient choreography
that has brought them here, something
as orderly and fated as sunrise, as simple
as the planets, and that now they will stroll happily
ever after into the sweet movie of their lives,
the light always at a perfect angle to the camera,
the beasts always trumpeted out from the brush
at the perfect moment, the obstacles
reshaping themselves like a boy's hand
placed under a blanket to amuse a kitten.
For months, maybe for years, they go on like this—
munching jackfruit in some beautiful tropic,
stalking the wild mushrooms of some pristine forest,
until they become the myth of themselves
they have been so long making,
the stars of their own enterprise,
and when life turns its dimmed lights up
once again and the theater empties,
they find the stranger love always delivers up

to the desperate, they see, at last, the reel
never shown at the theater—the one where
no music plays in the background, no blossom
rides the stem of the plucked flower,
and no face looks back at the smitten lover
but his own—hungry as it ever was, hungry
to reach back into the darkness, now, for real.

For/Against

I. For

Things that you're for are easy to explain—
they're what you're here for, more or less,
and so they stand for something, they're not
for naught, that's why you speak for them,
for better or worse: for kindness, love,
the things flesh says to flesh as flesh grows
speechful by and by, and you're for brotherhood,
for peace, you're for a better world than this
though this one's yours, and you're for salt,
for air, for late-night bourbon in some dark café,
you're for the weeds and flowers, and you're
for light, above all else, because it lovelies
what it sees, including you, and you're
for loveliness, however it may come. You're
for the animals and plants, the wild ones
most of all, since you're for wildness
in yourself as well, for what's untamed
when all grows civil in the end, you're for
the end, in fact, however it may come,
for what it means to know what we are for,
just for the hell of it if nothing else,
for rich or poor—we're here for that.

II. Against

Against romance, I say, 'cause I'm against
whatever sucks the life from what I'm for:
against the rich, against the dark, against
the sense that everything is equal in the end,
against all hatred, though I hate, against inversions

where the old bury the young, the sad the glad,
against frugality and impotence and rage,
(though I've been frugal, impotent and mad
at times myself), against Marcos, Duvalier
and Jesse Helms, against intelligence
that flattens down the heart, against the cruel.
I'm dead against the rain when rivers flood,
against the cold where children have no clothes,
old folks no heat. I've been against the very things
I'm for, when context sets the things I'm for
against themselves. Against this poem,
I would have been for silence many times
if I were wise, against my own stupidities
I write, against the absence of the things
I'm for, against my empty bed, against
my life, that cannot tell, at times,
what it has done, and why, as if it were
against and for at once its own dumb sake.

Death of a Romantic

But he did not shoot himself, and did not hang himself; he went on living.

—Tolstoy, *Anna Karenina*

Now I have entered into the general sadness
of my frail species, having come
to the dark corner of my own life,
the harsh mid-point at which the self
loses the previous grandeur of the self
and the high, rarefied air of solitude
comes to resemble, merely, a loneliness.
I look out over the grey-green waters
and watch the buoys bob with the bounties
of their traps, I feel the dock rise and lower
with the tides, and, whatever it is
I have always prayed to, I pray to again,
because it has come to resemble a habit,
because it is the one transit from the life I have lived
to the one I am moving toward, because I see now
that even the silence is a kind of continuum,
that we shall all come in the end to a place
of our own making, that the voice
which has always answered these prayers
is answering still.

▲▲▲ II ▲▲▲

CIVILITIES

Love should make joy; but our benevolence is unhappy.

—EMERSON

Good Intentions

They are what we always begin with:
the bright smile, the proffered light, the dreams
at the focal point of sleep, the casual fuck,
if fuck were such a thing. Always the air is large
with overtures of kindness, always the water
is smooth when the yachts set sail, but things
break up into their component parts—
the dinghys scuttle again toward shore,
the sails luff to remember wind
when it subsides, the skimmed milk
of romance settles in the glass
and we're alone with the pure
impurities of self and mottled light—
The birds no longer arrive to vindicate
the field guides, the stars no longer fall
into perfect constellations for the sake
of the astronomers, and the one perfect refrain
of life is life itself: the prologue done,
the glasses clicked, the introductions made
and cordials drunk, and kindness
for our only rule, if we were kind.

Manners

Just because a man pulls out your chair for you
and takes your coat at an elegant restaurant
is no guarantee that he really loves you. You know this,
and so whether he burps or farts over the dinner
like some sort of Chinese compliment
does not much matter to you, whether he subscribes
to the high sanctimony of the right thing
leaves you unmoved and lonely. Once,
like a Turkish princess, you were feted and dined
by all sorts of mannerly people, in a high castle
on the cliffs of Scotland. Now, so many thank-yous
and sincerelies later, it's the things unsaid,
the warm rudities of late night, that most move you
and you are wild for slurped sounds of the truly decent,
the I-chew-with-my-mouth-open look of the one
you will love forever. Whatever it is that might be said
for the predictable thing, the good manners
you were taught in childhood, it's more and more
the case of the auspicious oddity that excites you now,
the cool flippancy of the one who invents
his own decencies. *Darling,* I say to you,
fall to the floor all you want, I ain't pulling
chairs out for anyone. But what I'll whisper to you later,
in the orderly dark that comes every night like a good butler,
will be sweeter than all that, believe me,
something you can write home to mom about
as if I were the man who had sent you a dozen roses
on Valentine's Day, or smiled in the pretty picture,
or paid you the most beautiful compliment in the world—
only more slovenly, baby, more kind.

What a Time!

To dance, at a dark party, to old tunes
is not really to move: It's like chatter
at a long table, all in vain, and the moon
rising elsewhere. But it shakes up the bladder,

Yes it does, and though your lovely partner
may indeed be your wife, wouldn't it be nice,
you say to yourself, to dance with his, smarter
maybe than yours is, but not as lovely: no sunrise

In *her* eyes to be sure. And look how easily
lust glides through these rooms, the discs
still turning with their dark, oiled, breezy
calm against the turntable. No one here risks

Anything if they'll just leave early, keep
their eyes on their spouses, and moderate
their drinking. Soon they will all be asleep.
In fact, already he's whispering: *Dear, it's late,*

Which means, in French, *Quelle tristesse*
habite les heures du soir! Quel dommage!
And yet you know the truth: you're blessed
to be here, in this converted garage,

Wasting the evening in such syncopated style,
dancing to music you never liked, even then,
kissing your wife's white neck, all the while
dreaming of his, remembering how it was when

You were young, flamboyant, brazenly single
among the carefully arranged candles
and doctored punch. How you could mingle
then! But now, you'd like to have a handle

On your passions, or so you think. In your maturity,
you're nice to everyone, hardly ever sexual;
evenings, alone with friends, espouse the purity
of marriage. Would, now, you weren't so textual

In your resolve: You could move quietly, to Martha
and the Vandellas, into the dark, adjacent room
with your friend's wife, remembering your father
who, quoting Nietzsche re women and doom said:

Carry a large stick. You're the new norm now,
though: detailed and calm, all high monogamous.
You know desire, in the end, is hardly ever amorous,
yeah man, and off you bop into the night, transformed.

Garments

Now the sun's yellow smock is falling again
from the heavens. It is night. The nurse
is taking off her white uniform,
the policeman is tearing off his badge
and his blue hat, the doctor
is silently pulling the stethoscope
from around his neck. Slowly, button
by terrible button, people are undoing
the chrysalis of quotidian robes—
the dentist unfastening his plaque-ridden bib,
the chimney sweep flinging his soot-drenched shirt
into a corner, the bellhop emptying money
from his beleaguered pockets. The boards
of the world's floors grow heavy again
with a huge flotsam of bankers' suits,
the unleavened airiness of dancers' leotards.
Even the President we have all loved
for the sheer tedium of his sartorial sense,
yes, even he, is returning his body now
to the high ornament of its original suit,
even the talk-show host is unclipping
the microphone from his lapel, the seductress
peeling the frilled underwear from her body
by her own hand. We are becoming, like it
or not, a kind of democracy. We are all
growing equal beneath the naked moon.
We are all going to sleep, now, in the same bed.

Academic Suppers

Once there were twelve bodies
where we now sit. I know it,
because there are still husks
where those bodies once were,
empty carapaces
overtaken during the mind's coup,
begun as a benevolent dictatorship
but now gone wild
(as all power does)
with its sense of itself,
and so we are all seated here, captives
of bad wine and too much to eat,
and grow quietly to hate one another
for the pure tedium of what we have become—
repeating the word *tenure*
as if it were a mantra,
while the body,
that old anthropologist
(the one true scholar among us),
stirs restlessly
in its prison of pomp and conceptions,
as if to remind us
how brief its tenure is,
how transient its publications.

Charm

It issues, as all song does,
from some terrible emptiness, a hole
so deep it demands the oracular
to fill it, an amulet against evil
as its name suggests, so when a man
rises at a large party, full
as a linnet with his own music
and puffed with a seeming grandeur,
or a woman enters a room,
eyes so incantatory
even the curtains shudder from weakness,
we all know there is something
to be pitied in all that beauty,
something dead, perhaps, and transmogrified
as mulch and compost are, and that
what we are seeing is merely
the frail flower of some previous barrenness,
that the man or the woman will leave the room,
that very night, to become again
merely themselves—a wounded thing
yearning toward the light, a beautiful Carmen
serenading Escamillo, a darkness so deep
you can see its blackness right through
these compensatory lights,
such desperate flames.

To Each His Own

The two people discussing the presidential campaign
  at the table beside me must love one another,

I'm absolutely certain, and it is the heat of their talk,
  the absolute passion of their argument as she

Moves closer to him across the table that convinces me
  of the marvelous diversity of what we are,

That a savage heat rises in a disparate way from each
  country, and so I am reminded as I sit here alone,

Having dinner at the Harvest Restaurant in Cambridge,
  Massachusetts, that our lives are a constant

Mystery, a penumbra of conflicting desires that shimmer
  like fruit in the wild Jell-O of the body, and yes,

Friends, we could *all* be here at this restaurant on this
  night in late August, darkness lengthening

Like the arms of young boys during adolescence, and so
  strangely choreographed would be our desires,

Our manner of uttering them, that we might know, at last,
  how human an animal we all are, we might gesture,

Each in his own way, to the waiter for the check, and we
  would become then, in the small minutiae of acts

That constitute our day, beings thrust into the world—
  a sequestered spirit calling out from its warm box

Its syllables of chagrin and longing and harsh necessity.
  But soon, once again, the night will be over,

The birds will have fallen asleep again in their trees,
  the squelched perambulations of the earthworms

Will take their place, each of the wildly chattering people
  will have returned his voice to its sepulchral nest,

And the world will be again a place of perfect serenity:
  each muttering his intimacies across the table,

Each calling out to the garçon of evening in his own voice.

Civilities

for Daniel Jacobs

If you are too shocked by the sound of the psychiatrist
in the three-piece suit saying the words *blow job,*
it may be you have an overly refined sense of
the mock-decencies dress contains, that you have,
once again, underestimated the equalizing power of pleasure
and have lost, by an act of your own will, your sense
of the wild equipage against death all men hold.
It may be, in fact, that you have forgotten how—beneath
the humdrum distinguishments of finery and manners—
a standard incivility roams, the insistent cock
among a bevy of hens that must always be heard from,
and that the placid decencies a day extracts from us
are purchased at a price some darkness pays for, something
that must be uttered somewhere, to someone, perhaps
in a dark alleyway beneath the railroad trestle,
or on a couch somewhere, hidden from clear view, but
nonetheless urgent, needing to come into desire's
equalizing air, to deflate, once more, the *Verboten*
by the wild, syllabic thrust of its mere saying and to
remind us how mixed this place is in which we have
found ourselves, how strangely situated between doing
and thinking, between desire and the small fruitions
of desire we are sometimes capable of, between
proprieties and yet other proprieties which seem, at first,
unspeakable, but are only, in the end, the dark side
of some predictable decency, as speech is merely
the shadow side of silence—that final decency
all speech comes to in the end, pardon my saying so.

The Artichokes of Midnight

*Durable and life-giving inventions—tragedy, restaurants that stay open late at
night, holding hands, the edible artichoke—were probably half-discovered and
half-invented from the materials the world makes available.*

—Robert Haas

Late night at a dimly lit table, and yet another tragedy
of the will's helplessness. Whose small and eager hands
beckon from these windows, so sweet and edible
in their seeming? And what wild, splotched invention
of your own imaginings might you find here—an artichoke
leafed with its own hungers, as if in the cheap restaurant

Of desire you'd find contentment. But whose restaurant
is this, anyway? Does anyone think it a lesser tragedy
to live with someone, wedged like two artichokes
in a double boiler, than to carve with your own hands
the small, deliberate hurts of your own invention?
Oh, the will to have everything, to reduce to an edible

Compost of easiness the dark complaints, the incredible
longings of late night, as if life were a drive-thru restaurant
and you were merely the ravenous man who'd invented
melancholy! But even here, you see, life's not all tragic:
Occasionally, it's true, a man or woman dies by their own hand,
but then there are days when your life opens like an artichoke

At an elegant dinner, something no art you know can choke
the life out of. And a woman you once knew, so edible
and lovely you could hardly see her, took you by the hand,
led you out of that cold, damp, uninspiring restaurant
you were seated at, and told you: *Relax, life's no tragedy
unless you make it one, so why in God's name invent*

False miseries? It was that night, you think, you invented
the myth of your own life, sucking it like an artichoke

35

from its own roughage, treating it like any other tragedy
you hadn't ordered, detested, were trying to make palatable
as if it were a dish served to you in an elegant restaurant
you couldn't separate from its embellishments, but handled

And devoured like some primitive quadruped whose hands
served any purpose they arrived at, before the invention
of utensils and manners. *What kind of crazy restaurant
was that, anyway?* you asked her, holding the artichoke
up to the moonlight, wanting your life made cozy and credible
just by her answering. *Calm down,* she said, *it's not so tragic.*

So, hand in hand, you left the restaurant. Yet it's incredible
to you, that night: her warm hands and the scent of artichokes
reverberant still. And the making of tragedy: your own invention.

L'Addition

Always pay; for first or last you must pay your entire debt.
　　　　　　　　　—EMERSON, "Compensation"

You will pay for the long-legged waitress
in the tight black skirt, and you will pay
for the bars of Vivaldi in the relaxing lounge.

You will pay for the prisms of light
from the old chandeliers, and you'll pay
for the organdy wallpaper and fluted cloths.

You will pay for the Doric columns
and the wide chairs of teak, and you will pay
for the ice in your daiquiri and the salt on your rim.

You will pay for the dimmed lights
and the bright lights and the
bayberried fumes. And you'll pay
for the bourboned cigars and the artichokes of wax.

You will pay for the waiter's bright smile,
and you'll pay for the filigreed coatrack
and thinly sliced cheese.

Ah friends! Ah friends! What a life!—
You pay and you pay,
and you will pay again.

For a Friend, Having Abandoned
All He Once Stood For

At first I thought it was envy
that brought me to this—the infinite variety
of things to add to the bathwater, the dull drone
of the Jacuzzi against the wind, this room
for your unborn child, so perfectly choreographed
biology itself seems a kind of slippage,
the whole house, in fact, shuddering
with the things that have bought you, arranged
so perfectly that all life's beautiful confusion
has been edited out of it. Like an embodied silence,
it comes between us, a blunted tool stifling words
I once heard from you and believed to be yours.
And it *is* envy: so great a lust for the small immunities
the thinged life gives that I wanted to be you,
so wild a longing for the remoteness of your seeming
that I dream, in the next life, of changing places.
Yet it's the things things stand for that make us
mute here: your house, with its embellishments
of conformity and purpose, your wife,
with her sad ice of antithetical desires,
your child, that will wean its way like a lisp
into the perfect sentence of all you hope for.
Until all envy leaves me. *Things,* said Emerson,
are in the saddle, and ride mankind.

They are riding you, old friend.

They are riding us all.

Renovations

Because you have wanted both a woman and a house
that are in move-in condition, you have lived,
for many years now, alone, in rented apartments,
and you are tired of them. You are tired
of the deep perfection of other people's walls,
you are tired of the impeccable woman
your mind wakes up to, but your body lacks,
you are tired, in fact, of the whole world
of the other thing, the perfected structures
which are never in need of repair because
they are never there, and you are tired,
in the end, of your own relentless demands
for a better life. So you have come now
to a house of embellishable walls, a woman
of imperfect skin, you have seen in the mirror
your own imperfect face, the cracked image
of your own illusions. Slovenly with dirt,
you rise into the whole house of what is
imperfectly yours, grit-covered in the half light,
and you scrape from its improvable walls
the old paint, the green stuccoed swirls
of some previous possession. *Darling,*
you say to yourself, *this is the thing you own,*
and you are grateful for it. And, as you climb down
from the ladder that has lifted you
into your own small version of heaven, the door opens,
and a woman who is almost beautiful, but somewhat
in need of repair, walks into the house: merely a part
of the old half-happiness that is yours, now,
for the duration—as long, that is, as paint holds,
and mortar, and such vulnerable stone.

Suburban

Conformity caught here, nobody catches it,
Lawns groomed in prose, with hardly a stutter.
Lloyd hits the ball, and Lorraine fetches it.

Mom hangs the laundry, Fred, Jr., watches it,
Shirts in the clichéd air, all aflutter.
Conformity caught here, nobody catches it.

A dog drops a bone, another dog snatches it.
I dreamed of this life once. Now I shudder
As Lloyd hits the ball and Lorraine fetches it.

A doldrum of leaky roofs, a roofer who patches it,
Lloyd prowls the streets, still clutching his putter.
Conformity caught here, nobody catches it.

The tediumed rake, the retiree who matches it,
The fall air gone dead with the pure drone of motors
While Lloyd hits the ball, and Lorraine just fetches it.

The door is ajar, then somebody latches it.
Through the hissing of barbecues poets mutter
Of conformity caught here, where nobody catches it.
Lloyd hits the ball. And damned Lorraine fetches it.

The Letting

for Michael Ross

Minute and particular, arm strapped
to a wooden table in Memorial Hall
as a graphite cloud shuttles westward
on this damp day in the Year of Our Lord
nineteen hundred and eighty-six,
as the same serum I give now
streams down the face of a young Haitian
beaten by police, as the gathered flotsam
of seven terrestrials is culled from the sea
and a black South African boy squats
at the shebeen's edge to wait for his father,
I grieve in this small way for my kind as I
lie here, blubbered with sugar and good care,
a mere integer of flesh and selfishness,
a man strapped to a table, surrounded
by sweet-scented girls in blue smocks
and red crosses who will offer me donuts and coffee
when I am done, who will hand me a thin brochure
in which all risk is rendered palpable
and explicit, so that I can serenely bleed
in this small way for my kind, while my kind
bleeds back   bleeds back   bleeds back   bleeds back

▲▲ III ▲▲

THE ART
OF POETRY

*I can so well remember the first time Gertrude Stein took me
to see Guillaume Apollinaire. It was a tiny bachelor's apart-
ment on the rue des Martyrs. The room was crowded with a
great many small young gentlemen. Who, I asked Fernande,
are all these little men. They are poets, answered Fernande.
I was overcome. I had never seen poets before, one poet yes
but not poets.*

—GERTRUDE STEIN,
The Autobiography of Alice B. Toklas

▼▼▼▼▼▼▼▼▼▼▼▼▼▼▼▼▼▼▼▼▼▼▼▼▼▼▼▼▼▼▼▼▼▼▼▼▼

The Tip of the Iceberg

Say language really does what it says it does:

That the bird in your hand
is really a bird, that it takes two
to tango, that whoever digs
his own grave will have to sleep in it.
Say you have a fool for a friend,
feckless and dissipated and greedy
beneath the stars, and that it takes one
to know one. Say that might
makes right, that the best offense
is a good defense, that fools rush in
where trepid angels stammer
in front of the doormats. Say
that life's unfair, that that's
the way it is, that someone tells you
"Have a nice day" and really means it.
What would it be like: the word,
reticent and calm, urged out
once more toward its true meaning?
What would it mean if "till death
do us part" really meant *till all breath
leaves me, love;* if "forever" meant
until the tides cease? What would it signify
if "love" could only mean *love* once more,
not just the tip of the iceberg, sinking,
and in all sincerity.

The Word *Love*

Anarchical, monosyllabic, wild
with a plethora of resonances so vast
they threaten to engulf us,
it moves out over the world,
part shadow and part dream, part
of the living *res* itself,
yet so filled
with the echo of its own longings
it becomes, in this way, the crux
of our long failure with language—
co-opted by the movies, guilt-ridden,
marketed like a commodity—until,
as de Tocqueville says, we thud
into our times, splotched things
language has its way with, puppets
and puppeteers of the tongue's meanderings,
while even this—the one clear thing
we all thought we wanted when we thought
what we wanted would respond to thought—
becomes an unclarified blur,
yet one more fatality of the sense
we lost in trying to make sense, a word
I have uttered time and time again
and now hesitate to say at all—
being, as it is, always too much
to stand for what we really mean,
and never enough.

Trying to Learn Basketball at 37

Too late in the middle of mid-life,
I stand at the foul line,
feigning an ease that is not my ease,
imagining the cool swish of rubber
through the hoop as my ball arcs
like a wounded bird toward the net
and falls short time and time again.
Beside me, a girl who in my prime
would have been merely called *applause*
dribbles elegantly to her boyfriend's right
and wafts a jump shot with such perfect
parabolic glee against the fiberglass
and down through the rim
that I am awed out of my own envy
and pause to watch, and watch again
as she drives hard beneath the basket
and lays one up, elegant as a swan.
Her boyfriend, too, possesses the grace
of the right time and, patting her
like a teammate on the ass, fakes
to her left and glides,
on the clear ice only the body knows,
past flailing arms, and I am awed again
as the ball shakes like a pair of hips
through the net, and drops. Now,
I am reminded it was the love
of beauty that brought me here,
and I pause once more, all will
where thoughtlessness should live,
and dribble, cool as Cousy, toward the net,
setting the ball again to air,
watching it rise with the grim intensity

of a blind date, as it bashes
haplessly against the rim
and hunkers back. Poetry,
I console myself,
is a kind of basketball.

I can do that.

Seven O'Clock Muse

She is not Walter Cronkite, though she is beautiful
and has been with you all of your life. Perhaps
she will come to you tonight from Tel Aviv or Cairo,
from a small town in Iowa, ravaged by pestilence
or ice storms. Or perhaps she'll arrive at midnight,
captioned for the deaf, repeating herself
as you lie in the bed, considering the smallness
of events, the dull order of significance.
She is pure American, the voice of a country
your parents fled to without really wanting it,
some strange democracy you now inhabit
and have grown to love easily. She will tell you
tonight that this is your life, these words
and the beautiful patterns they fall in on the page,
ordering the world for you, singing you to sleep,
always reminding you: *That's the way it is.*

Stamps

after Bruno Schultz

They are the world's licked emissaries—
serpents and volcanoes, presidents, flotillas
of rare birds, passerine and pelagic, that glide
over oceans, bundles of greeting clasped
in their claws, and they are what acquaints us,
in serrated scenes of never-seen places,
with what the exotic is: azure archipelagos
and distant marshes, parrots that cry out:
Guatemala, Guatemala, pink seas that arch
over their inlets like young girls' slips
and then fade into beaches of lava. Small
fragile things, collected by those we once found
eccentric, they are welcomed into our lives now ·
as a kind of testimony to people, places,
dreams we might otherwise have forgotten,
birds from exotic countries: small griefs
and gallinules fluttering over deep waters,
trying to mean.

A Modern Poet

The corpse was hardly cold but that the dutiful son
had already written a sonnet of bereavement
concerning his great loss and this and that, and Oh
what an onslaught of emotion it was: complete
with black flowers and penitence and the like,
which he immediately sent off, enclosing a stamped,
self-addressed envelope, to a little magazine
in the Midwest that was doing a special issue
entitled, simply, *Loss*, where it won for him
The Lenore G. Tearsworthy Poetry Prize: three
hundred dollars and a reading tour of seventeen
Midwestern colleges. What comfort, he thought,
remembering Wordsworth, lies in the mere
utterance of grief, why he felt better already.

And so the moral of the story—

Grief needn't be that deep for us to grieve:
It can hurt just to write what we'd like to believe.

The Pleasures of Abstraction

The imperfect is our paradise.
    —WALLACE STEVENS

There are poems written against abstraction: beauty
Lives in them only in the particular pleasures
They provide in their lines: the happiness
Of a pear or a wicker basket, the irrefutable truth
Of a footprint in the snow. There is a small justice
In this reign of the tangible: more amenable than love

To our desire for constancy, more democratic than our love
Of the grand gesture, yet a kind of serene beauty
Lives in such small things, a hedge against injustice,
So that, each time we return to them, they provide a pleasure
We can rely on, a revealed shard of the world's larger truths,
And we can return, then, to our quest for the large happiness,

Relieved, at least in part, if not perfectly happy,
Knowing we are surrounded by the things we love—
A silk lampshade, a filigreed coatrack; things, to be truthful,
We hadn't appreciated when their unpretentious beauty
Was first presented to us (even viewed with displeasure),
But now take as a measure of the world's true justice,

An amalgam of tangible equalizers distributed, not just
At random, but as if some divine sense of earthly happiness
Had been finally apprehended. There is no small pleasure
In saying this, for it posits again our craving for love
As something incarnate, graspable as a doorknob, beautiful
As an omelette, but no further removed from the truth

Than weather is, or the joys of the lepidopterist: considered true
Without our questioning it, of which we might say: *It just is,*

Shrugging our shoulders and turning to something of true beauty—
The Dog Star Sirius, say, or the thought of how truly happy
We once were, in our memory at least, when enduring love
Was not yet the issue, but the sensate cacophony of pleasures

We now think of as childish, but didn't then; when pleasure
Was its own large morality, when the tactile and the true
Were one, and we were assured, unconditionally, of the love
Of proximate bodies, an almost sociobiological justice
Which, because it preceded our quest for it, made us happy
In the banal sense but, in retrospect, still lends a beauty

To our recollections, a sense of pleasure and perfect happiness
Which, though it contradicts our experience of untruth and injustice,
Seemed a kind of absolute beauty then, a kind of love.

Advice to My Students:
How to Write a Poem

Forget, now, for a moment
that you were the blond boy
whose father jumped off the bridge
when you were only eleven. Forget
that you are the brokenhearted,
the cuckolded, the windswept lover
alone beneath the dangling pines.
Forget that you are the girl
of the godless cry, that no one
took you into his arms
during the cold night, that you have cried
from the fathomless depths
like a blue whale, and the world
has called back to you only its oracles
of relinquishment and moonlight.
Forget, now, my young friends,
everything you can never forget,
and hear, in the untamed wind,
in the perorations of the ravishing air,
the words for your life: *omelette,
divestiture, Prokofiev, stars.*
Forget, even as you gaze up at them,
the astral bodies and the heavenly bodies,
forget, even, your own ravenous body
and call out, into the beckoning light,
the names of everything you have
never known: flesh and blood, stone
and interlude, marmalade and owl—
those first syllables of your new world:
your clear and forgotten life.

Dancing with
a De-constructionist

She thinks I am only there
for her benefit, so,
when we move this way,
to old Motown and Rolling Stones,
it is as if there is no text at all,
and, though it seems to me it is *I*
who am leading *her* across the de-carpeted floor
of this apartment in East Cambridge,
there is in her eyes the glint of someone
alone with their best pleasure,
a solipsist of the highest order,
and it is as if she is looking right through me
into the wall, where large hieroglyphs
of motions I am not making lead her
to some fabulous beast, a wild subtext
taking her, better than I ever could,
to where she wants most to be. And so,
in a certain way, we are both happy:
I who think I am leading her along
to some rhythm she could not possibly find
on her own, and she who has seen through
this subterfuge of hips and legs
as if I were pure spirit—which is how,
in some way, I had wanted it all along . . .
and the Supremes and Rolling Stones
secretive among the speakers, taking it
all in, helping us to forget what it was
that brought us here to begin with.

Prayer to Be Recited
after a Jacques Derrida Lecture

By the word by this text begins . . .
             —FRANÇOIS PONGE

By the word *by* this text begins, dear God,
Whose first line tells the truth
Of all feeling, which is the truth
We pray you preserve against the lies
Of pure intellect, the neglect of the body.
You can surely judge for yourself, O
Lord, our difficulties, living here
In the dark of the mind's vengeance,
Where all that we once knew for certain
Has been de-constructed, and misfortune
Resonates backward from its initial text
To afflict its maker like a mirror
Broken seven years *after* the bad luck
It originally caused. Compassionate One,
Restore us, once more, to our original
Innocence, let the heart reassert itself
Through the dark of this intelligenced text.
Permit us to see, again, by the clear light
Of its original making. By the word *by*,
Dear God, return us to the hallowed ground
Of our text's first making. May we never forget,
Lord, what we were first moved by . . .

It Is Best Not to Sit at Your Desk
Too Long, but to Rise

for Yehuda Amichai

For if you will only walk out into the day,
there will be flakes of snow still on the hedges,
a diaspora of leaves, breasts
uprising against the dull awnings of their cups,
the flotsamed gatherings of last night, a mass
of garbage that has not yet risen into the air,
relinquished bottles and old stockings, chairs
that have contained the beautiful bottoms of generations,
convenings of miraculous grey pigeons and sparrows,
once-hopeful spirits that have passed yet another night
amid the wafted embrasure of heated gratings,
there will be rich men and poor men, and poor
beautiful women (and, yes, rich beautiful ones),
taking off for the odd callings of their various days,
there will be the young clerk who secretly studies Sanskrit
but who has risen early this morning
to sweep the meticulous floor of the jewelry shop,
there will be the fatty risings of butter
in the world's equalizing croissants (raspberry,
blueberry, chocolate, cheese), and there will be
those who have remembered your name (praise them)
and those who have already forgotten it
(praise them as well), and the desperate banker
who has just written a villanelle on the Green Line
and the desperate poet who has spent the whole night
dreaming of banks, and you can be there,
on the ordinary, thing-infested streets
of this life, happy as an epigraph, curious

as a peninsula—a mock-heroic thing
that struts along the streets of this life,
a voice looking for something to sing about:
a razzmatazz of hopes, a suckaboo of stars.

The New Yorker Poem

It is best to mention a painter,
but obliquely, not too early,
say, in the fourth line, as in:
She had a face like a Cézanne still life—
disproportionate, overpainted, painstakingly
orderly; to reveal, slowly and subtly,
your erudition, your eclectic intelligence,
your love of the natural world. A hint
of Wallace Stevens (flamboyantly singsong,
delightfully difficult, bilingual)
ought to appear somewhere *(She lit*
the contrapuntal darkness with her song,
quotidian, blemished, ein kleines Liebeslied
among the sceptered stars). Always
mention water *(the madefacting tears*
that washed like tide against her cheeks)
and wildflowers *(primrose, meadowsweet,*
blazing star). It is best if you are already
"someone" (they will pay you a substantial fee
for the mere pleasure of reading your poems),
but this need not deter you: It is enough
simply to *know* "someone," to have them send
a cover letter of their own along with your poem,
or, better yet, you might just get lucky:
Cézanne may yet appear to you
amid the contrapuntal darkness, reeking
of forget-me-nots and gentians, wafting
his dappled palette against the moon,
etching your reputation into the light,
but merely on paper—
quotidian and blemished and loved by everyone.

Brevities

I. Psychobiography of the Cheerful Poet

His life was fun, its analysis inductive:
He was a happy bard, but self-destructive.

II. Lust & Marriage

As in captivity the brilliant quetzal pales and dies,
Desire, married, flaps its wings but cannot fly.

III. The Poet's Consistency

Though once again his mind had changed, his friends all noted,
All that he'd said was true—until he wrote it.

IV. The Passionate Lovers

From their brief pleasures did much longer woes succeed:
They gobbled flowers when they should have planted seed.

V. Narcissus

Endowed with charm and irresistible good looks,
He had to learn from life what others learned from books.

VI. The Good Wife

She lost herself in him, she thought, at no great cost,
Only to wake, and find him found, and herself lost.

VII. Of Adam & Eve

Who, happy though they were, longed for a happier state
And reaching for the tray, destroyed the golden plate.

VIII. The Novice Bird-watcher

He heard the trilling call, then saw a dappled wing, slightly aflame,
And missed the lovely bird, while trying oh-so-hard to find its
name.

IX. A Successful Poet

Just as the blinded prophets would incant at night,
He now gives readings who once used to write.

X. A Brief History of Morality

How boring morals are, that only fell
From dying flesh recast beneath a dying spell.

XI. The Poet's Mistress

The songs he sang so catered to her needs,
She only heard his words, but missed his deeds.

XII. The Retired Poet

He fled the scene, because he had no choice—
Since he had found himself, but lost his voice.

XIII. The Poet's Estate

The only thing he knew for certain, but denied it:
All that he felt: divided, subdivided.

The Source

Because lack is what drove you to it
to begin with, because you were empty
and, wanting to fill yourself, spoke,
pushing air into the air, filling the silence
with a larger silence like an underground tunnel,
because loss cuts deeper than pleasure
and is unredeemable, you continue
beyond the initial need that brought you to it,
beyond the failure of anonymous love,
beyond the large aftervoid of applause,
you continue beyond the limits, even,
of your gifts, until there is nothing
left to do but repeat yourself (having said all
that you had to say), you continue beyond hope,
beyond pleasure, beyond the unrectifiable truth
that brought you here, for when the applause dies
and all the beautiful women have gone home
to the real bodies of inarticulate lovers,
all you can hear is the man at the back
of the auditorium, the one who resembles
yourself and is always whispering:
Never enough   Never enough.

▲▲ IV ▲▲

THE HEARTS
OF MEN

What is one man among so many men?
What are so many men in such a world?
Can one man think one thing and think it long?
Can one man be one thing and be it long?

—WALLACE STEVENS,
"The Comedian as the Letter C"

The Walkers of Hurricanes

I love the people who walk out in hurricanes,
who love the elements we must all join someday
more than the tepid flesh of their own bodies,
who love the wild graffiti the storm strews
over the streets and highways and immaculate yards
more than the pale order of the everyday,
who have tasted before the sweet fragrance
of their deaths, and lived to tell of it.
I love those strange pedestrians—the old
and young and seemingly timid, the mock-fragile ones
of the later years—who have turned off their television sets,
to defy the journalists and pundits and wild hysteria
of the meteorologists and wrapped themselves again
in the worn suitcases of reliable bodies, who have walked
down to the water to watch the wind race over
the storm's flotsam, to contemplate the beautiful confusion
of the gulls surrendering themselves to the crazed air,
to experience once more the calm relinquishment
of their earthly hubris, if for even a moment, as they listen,
now, to the sweet insistence of unearthlier powers,
as they weave through the downed signatures
of willow, horse chestnut, maple and fencepost,
as they walk past the taped windows and closed commerce
of quotidian light and grow grateful once more
for this bountiful life that has just swept them up—
that will sweep them away again with the same hand.

A Man Grieves Always
for the Ships He Has Missed

I believe in all sincerity that if each man were not able to live a number of lives beside his own, he would not be able to live his own life.

—Paul Valéry

So he goes, nightly, down to the docks
To wave at the glorious ships. He goes

Down to wave at the prows and the deckhands
And the sails that hang blowsy in the channel,

Because they have gone somewhere, anywhere,
Without him, because his life is an ongoing yelp

Against the singular self, because the shore
He lives on is never as lovely as the shore,

In another life, he might have sailed to.
He goes down and waves at the lives he could

Never have lived, so as, somehow, to make them
His own, because the grief of the never-taken roads

Is the grief of all men, because his one wife
Awaits him in the dark and his children, even now,

Dream into being their unlivable lives, because
He makes, as he does this, the one catwalk

He can build onto all these ships: those words
He utters time and time again—to his wife,

To his children, to anyone who will listen:
Here, above the raging sea: *his home.*

Skototropic

Skotos: (Gk.) darkness, gloom

A deep thing blazons toward its name to find relief,
And cold, in a mythic way, it moves through dark,

As if it knew the darkness has a bad name all in vain,
That a deep thing plunges in a deepened way toward light,

The way plankton move in darkness through the polyped deep,
The way a climber, on the dark side of a peak, moves first

Through caves, ravines, encampments of the shade; the way
The early hurts, in dark, release the rectifying urge

That sets the words to song to speak its name. It moves
Through dark, because the dark is there, because the dark

Describes a sense of light deferred, because it is
A taproot to the light, whose light is dark inverted

Just as prayer is song. It moves. It rests. It slithers
Toward its source, as if the dark could echo lightward

In a tethered way. And then, at last, it rises toward
The light—a kindled thing that rectifies its birth,

A burning that inflames all that it marks:
So dark a thing that moves it moves the dark.

Dr. Wuschti

Washington Heights, 1959

What we wanted most eluded us
and was unkind: Secretive as dew,
leaving his messages in back of our garbage trucks
the way a desperate mother, these days,
might leave an infant, he appeared
when we asked him to appear—
appointed to be ours for the day
as we roamed the streets, orphaned
as all boys are orphaned
when they turn to speak their father's name
and a mere man answers.

And so we walked those streets:
Audubon, Amsterdam, Pinehurst and Broadway,
each day some new stranger summoned to be ours—
small, in a grey coat, spectacled and thin,
or paunched, ill-fitted, lumbering and bald.
But always, in the end, *lost.* We were preparing,
I think now, for love: for whatever it is
that calls our name into the morning air
and we spend the rest of the day hot
on the heels of, only to lose once more
so that the game can continue. Men now,
we are still protagonists of the deep drama
those small boys wrote. And the games of childhood
utter out their passion to be real. And those boys
still roam the streets, calling *Wuschti*
Wuschti like hope to the prophetic air.

Lucky

Off to the market to buy a lottery ticket,
I consider the possibilities of luck: good luck,
bad luck, beginner's luck, hard luck, the luck
of the draw, and I realize I am lucky, in fact,
to be here at all, on this benignly lit street
on a night in October, as luck would have it,
and I know that it's not just the luck of
the Irish, but any man's, to walk the streets
of his town, beneath the shapely moon,
and ponder the dumb luck that brought him here,
against all odds, into the vast lottery of minnow
and ovum, and to know he has once again lucked out,
this very night, spent as it has been without
accident or incident, a small testimonial
to the quietudes that are still possible,
the only half-felt wish for some grand stroke
of luck that will change everything, that will
change, really, nothing at all, our lives being,
in some sense, beyond the vicissitudes
of luck and yearning, the night being lovely,
the day finite, many of those we know whose luck
has already run out, and we not yet among them,
thank the beneficence of Lady Luck, our stars
just now flickering into flame
as the night lucks in.

The Happy Nihilist

What's extraordinary's loving
where you are: the sparrow
creeping on the frazzled vine,
the cracks that undulate
around the table and the wall.

What's pleasanter
than sipping inexpensive wine . . .
the broken pipe, the unexpected call?

How many imperfections
can a day endure? Am I a bit
of smiling in a shoe? What's gentler
than a man in bed alone, a child
just now recovered from the flu?

The tragic hovers in the corners
of the house. It shivers
in the pillows and the sheets.
It winds its slender rope around
the half-completed and complete.

Why bother licking these half-empty plates?
Why drain the glasses in the sink?
Why mock the lonely minstrels at the gate,
the old girls elegant and homely in their minks?

Are we retarded in our daily rounds?
Are we just burning embers in the dust?
Are we the Deity's own lost and found?
I smile because I must.

The Hearts of Men

for Karen Allen

Swing
like pendulums
from rage to remorse,
from anger to shame.
They do not know
The smaller increments
of a gradual birth,
the gentler shocks
of a congruent light.
All eruption, they pour
their grief like tide
into the air
and move out again,
like Odysseus,
into the deep sea
of disconnectedness,
the wide berth
of their denials. Once,
loved for their weeping,
they were coddled like yolks
in some womanly forgiveness.
Then, they became
what all men become
to earn their one stifled syllable—
an instrument
so hampered in its range
it becomes a bellows,
so shortened in its stops
it resembles a trumpet.
What will they do now
who have gone so long
without weeping,

who seem to have lost forever
the gradual repertoire,
the harp and the flute,
the piccolo and pizzicato?
In whose name,
impoverished ones,
will they learn to love? Who
will embrace them once more
for the shaken trill
of their weeping—
their cleft, broken hearts?

Etymology Lesson
on the Road to Rome

The root words for passion
and for suffering are the same.
That's where desire leads you:
you suffer for it. So you try
no desire. The root word
for boredom's not the same,
but it might as well be—
you suffer as well.

So where does it lead you?—
Not just etymology is true;
No cliché takes us too far from home.
Both lust and its absence make us blue;
All roads lead, invariably, to Rome . . .

And it burns.

The Heart of Quang Duc

Saigon, 11 June 1963

When Quang Duc poured gasoline all over his body
in the streets of Saigon in 1963
and lit a match to it,
there was a large conflagration, flames
shooting in all directions at once,
the flesh charring, then sizzling,
then almost disappearing into the fire
as his body's two hundred and seven bones,
its seventy percent that is water,
contracted toward ash. All of Quang Duc
had been reduced to rubble, except
for his heart, which, like a phoenix,
rose from the small bucket of ash intact
and was thought by his fellow Buddhists
to be an omen of all that survives
a mere man's death. Twice more
they lit the dead man's heart, hoping
to send it after him. Twice more
it would not burn, twice more it refused
to enter its master's dwelling,
as if to say: *Not yet, not yet,*
I will not follow. But the third time
they poured fuel over the dead man's heart
and set it aflame, the heart joined itself
to the heat of that earlier fire, and,
like a pig's fat roasting on a spit,
sizzled into the afternoon, and was gone.
The Buddhists and Christians watched silently
as Quang Duc's heart sputtered into the air.
They knew they were learning something
that would serve them throughout the war—

that no man's heart
can survive more than three burnings,
that nothing can beat through fire
forever, or for very long.

The Man Who Needed No One

He wanted to need no one, not
love or thirst, not even sunrise
and the sweet amulets of water
that fall from the heavens.

No, he wanted to be an island
of self-sufficiency, to sleep
with his arms around the pillow,
a jack-in-the-pulpit alone on his throne
in the damp woods, singing to himself
beneath his curled umbrella.

And this is how he lived for many years—
a solitary song, a soliloquy
spoken into the small mirror
that hung above the wash basin,
with its blue towel and basket of dead flowers.

But something remained wrong—
a dull ache whispered from below his voice
where his heart should have been, a seed
rumbled in the pit of his stomach as if to suggest
a tree that had never grown, a stone skimming
the surface of water once and then sinking.

He grew old this way, never knowing
it had been need he had needed all along—
the sound of his own small voice
asking for a light to see by, a match
to retrieve his heart with from the widening dark.

The Scullers

They move the way love moves, or ought
to move, or did move once before The Fall,

But still they move this way, as if the ages
of gold and bronze had never left us, and so

They glide out into the gilded light, wedded
on both sides to the same stroke, pulling in

To push the water out, ratcheting their arms
into the late light as they sail, frictionless

As birds, to where the river turns like an elbow
into dusk, and they must know what they know,

Dear God, without words, they must know as
lovers knew before they knew what they knew,

And theirs must be the world again as we unmade
it—when dusk turned, as it does now, the color

Of iron, basest of the metals, and swallowed
the scullers toward grey in all our names.

Trip to Bountiful

It is good to have someone to sit beside
late at night, at the movies
when the lights have dimmed
and the previews are over
and you have pigged out over a large order of popcorn,
and the old woman who has lived unhappily
for twenty-one years with her failed son
and her miserable daughter-in-law takes off
to return to that beautiful small town
where she has always remembered herself
as perfectly happy, only to find
that her one friend, the town's last citizen,
has died that very morning, and that when she returns
to the beautiful house that has remained unaltered
in the scrapbook of her wishfulness,
it is a mere ghost of what it once was,
the curtains rotted against the sashes,
the wood frame sagging like an old scarecrow,
the neighbors' houses all abandoned
by death, ice storms, the vicissitudes
of profit; yes, it is good not to be alone
at times like these, when the woman
sitting beside you (who this very morning
seemed merely a burden) sends small sobs
wafting like pollen into the theater
and squeezes your hand, and says "It's
so sad, this movie," and you agree, yes,
it is very sad, this movie, and this life
in which so much we imagine as inalterable
will be taken from us, in which
there are so many towns where someone
will die, this very day, alone and unclaimed

by any of their loved ones (who have all left
to marry in another country or find their fortunes
in some greed-stricken Houston)
which is why it is good to be here,
even just tonight, in this dimly lit theater,
with a good woman and the scent of popcorn
and a wide bed you can climb into again together,
as if it were the town you originally came from
and you could always go back to it,
as if no one could ever die in the dark alone,
not even you.

The New Story of Your Life

Say you have finally invented a new story
of your life. It is not the story of your defeat
or of your impotence and powerlessness
before the large forces of wind and accident.
It is not the sad story of your mother's death
or of your abandoned childhood. It is not,
even, a story that will win you the deep
initial sympathies of the benevolent goddesses
or the care of the generous, but it is a story
that requires of you a large thrust
into the difficult life, a sense of plenitude
entirely your own. Whatever the story is,
it goes as it goes, and there are vicissitudes
in it, gardens that need to be planted,
skills sown, the long hard labors
of prose and enduring love. Deep down
in some long-encumbered self,
it is the story you have been writing
all of your life, where no Calypso holds you
against your own willfulness,
where there are no longer dark caves
for you to be imprisoned in,
where you can rise
from the bleak island of your old story
and tread your way home.

▲▲ V ▲▲

STILLNESSES

I said to my soul, be still, and wait without hope
For hope would be hope for the wrong thing; wait
*   without love*
For love would be love of the wrong thing, there is
*   yet faith*
But the faith and love and the hope are all in the
*   waiting.*
Wait without thought, for you are not ready for
*   thought:*
So the darkness shall be the light, and the stillness
*   the dancing.*

—T. S. ELIOT, "East Coker"

So sure of victory at last is the courage that can wait.

—MARK TWAIN,
"The Private History of a Campaign That Failed"

▼▼

The Mountains of Evening

All we have done to the wild heart
lives here. It is an architecture

Of severe sadness, a minstrel song
that whinnies and glides over the hills,

Tendering the trees, felling the prosperous
drifts of snow that have humped their way

Up over the rivulets of mud and grass
above the tree line, over the night-hoverings

Of the swallows and juncos. Whoever
has slept here has slept so silently

(Hardly a breath umbering out into the
star-drenched heavens, hardly a trill

With which to awaken the serpents
and dragonflies) that even the soft,

Oracular flutes of the angels can be
heard against the leapt constellations,

Even the unflicked tongue of night is raveling
its dark harvest against the landscape. Someday,

Free of the earth, free of its profligate
expenditures of daylight and evening,

These mountains will rise of their own accord
and flee from the landscape. They will lift

On some night just like this one, away
from the root-bound trees, lumbering up

Toward the beckoning flames of the planets,
hurdling their shoulders against the stars,

Proposing their own dark names to the night
and the galaxies and the ravenous heavens.

The Lovers Sleep Late
on Sunday. It Is Good.

Why should they not share
    their pleasures
with the sheets? The jays
    caw. Grackles flutter
like tinsel onto the grass.
    Tupelos blush

In the brisk air of autumn
    and, deep in their
mulched-over dens, foxes
    flame like lust
into the dark. O indolence,
    whoever gave you

Your bad name, what did they
    know about the body?
Against ash, against melancholy
    they climb one another
like good vines and rise, finally,
    toward the windows,

The women brushing their hair,
    the men planning,
already, their wild escapes
    though, for a moment,
all is the seeming peace of clutch
    and kiss. And now the world

Echoes to a cacophony of lips
    as, trembling, the bodies
turn for a final time between
    the sheets—like a prayer
on an infidel's lips, a flame
    that is about to go out.

Grace

Outside my window, maple leaves loom large
and the brief attention scatters
through the cracked glass and the screen
into a circle of sunlight between the trees.
In this clear, June cathedral of New Hampshire,
out from the eye's sight but not the mind's,
you stand in your studio, in the two o'clock light,
mixing the mauve and the lavender, watching
the light seep through the glass and the ferns,
with their Caravaggio of names *(maidenhair,
spleenwort, cliffbrake, horsetail)*, sway
beside the bluewhites and lady's slipper.

Through the woods not far away, a woman,
your wife, squeezes paint onto her palette.
She raises a cup of coffee to her lips and,
as she does, you think of her and of Bonnard,
and how, this morning, light fell like grace
upon her hair. And you realize that all gifts,
even grace, are purchased by the dull waiting,
by the lonely, bearded man who sits between us
in his cold room and stares, for hours,
without moving, at the silent keys, only staring,
staring, the way a man stares at the ivory skin
of a woman who will never be his.

And then, suddenly, he is like the blind man in Maine
returned to his eyes by a lightning storm: His hands
fly over the keys in a song that is mauve and lavender,
incarnadine and burnt sienna, and he realizes
grace is the constant incipience, the open field
and the good smoke rising; it is the long wait

for the red-eyed vireo and not the backward glance
of Orpheus; it is the passage through the dark tunnel
and the long silence before the empty canvas,
the blank page, and the mute, beautiful keys,
and, finally, the moment when the word,
the paint, and the mad fingers of the possessed
fly over the keys and the woods reverberate
with the tones and brushstrokes of grace
making its way joyfully through the dark tunnel
into the long, graceful arms of these magnificent fields.

The Analysand

for Sacvan Berkovitch

He wanted to know the truth,
to be free, at last,
of the world of illusion
in which he had felt himself,
for so long, a prisoner.
He wanted to know the *real* birds,
the *real* nature of love and hate,
the myths behind the myths.
He wanted a world so pure,
so untainted in its truthfulness,
a world in which the eating of all fruits,
the plunder of all trees,
was permissible, part
of the hegemony of his race.

So he lay, for years,
on the cold couch,
and, brick by brick,
tore down the house
of his illusions, he tore down
the walls and the floors,
the roof and the windows,
he tore down the doors,
and, finally, he tore
at the foundation itself,
hoping a place without illusion
would reveal itself there.

He wanted to build a new house,
a house that would survive
illusion, a house
all of whose materials

would be some form of truth.
But the deeper he dug,
the more earth he moved,
the more walls he tore down,
he found only new layers of illusion—
never a pure bird, but only
the sound of birds, never the pure light,
but only the texture of light,
never the perfect truth, but only
another illusion of truth.

Until, finally, he grew tired
of tearing down the old house,
he grew tired of digging
beneath the old foundation,
and he found he needed
a place to live in. He found
that the illusion of cold
was a real cold, the illusion
of fatigue, a real fatigue.
So he gathered, bit by bit,
the pieces of the old house,
he gathered the stones
of the illusory foundation,
the glass of the illusory windows,
he replaced the old roof
as protection against
the illusory ice storms, the heat
of the pure light he'd longed for.

But this time he felt
there was a kind of truthfulness

to the illusory house—
the glass seemed more real,
the wood more consoling,
he felt that the bed he slept on
had grown more comfortable.
And finally he realized
he had begun to like
the illusions he could live with—
the imaginary birds, the invented
wind. He had grown tired
of looking so hard
for the unsullied truth—

As if truth were the one thing a man could look for.
As if truth were something that could feed or clothe you.
As if truth were as truthful as love's illusions . . .

As if truth were a merely human thing to know.

Somewhere Else

"Isn't it great to be somewhere else?"
  —AN AIRLINE PASSENGER

"My giant goes with me wherever I go."
  —EMERSON

Someday in your life it will come,
that time when you can no longer escape
the sheer sheerness of your singular selfhood,
when the good bird you have been chasing all these years
finally descends onto your own two shoulders
and the animals who have escaped from the barn
(the cows, the sheep, your one good goat)
suddenly return there, and a terrible dread
comes over you at first, and then a relief
at having come to the one, half-abysmal possibility
of your own being, like the good dwarf
that will grow no further. Yes, someday
it will come, when you have traveled
to some southernmost peninsula
where the land juts like a worn thumb
into the sea and you can go no further
on the low ground that is the fruit of your making,
Yes, this too shall come, at some difficult turn,
and, when you emerge from it, it shall seem
as if the body of flesh were the metaphor of all light
on which the dark bird of love has come home to roost,
and the city of angels shall be the city of dust,
and the dreams of the young child who flew
and the man who fell from the uprootedness of air
shall be one, and nowhere will be somewhere
and the else a you.

Stones in Love

These unembellished faces can conceal
A heart of gold, I'm told by those
Who've lived with stones and ought to know.
Their sullen, inward eyes don't glow
In the dark and, though not bold
In amorous matters, they're known to steal

Away at night, to no one's gaze,
I've heard it said, to hug and kiss
Below the dunes, against the level sands.
And friends have seen them holding hands
In dark cafés, along a lightly traveled place,
Rhapsodic in their stone-faced bliss.

And why, dear friends, should we deny
To stones, who pave our ways, who line
The flues of our seductive places,
The joys of love? For their blank faces?
Because theirs is a reticence divine?
Because, unlike ourselves, they will not die?

Winter Solstice, 1983

I ponder the complexity of things:
how the sun moves, azimuthal,
through the weave of sky,
how the wintered days deplete the air
of light, how a broken thing
replenishes its bleeding scars
until its life becomes an elegy to what it knows.
Last night, I dreamt my way into a better life:
the trees were lichened to the air,
the paths toward wisdom weren't obtuse,
the words men utter in the haste of heat
did not take years to utter back.
I woke as men wake all their days—
distempered by the conflict of their wish
and ways, beleaguered by the antique griefs
that cling like oak leaves through the cold.
But I grow wise, at last, remembering
the early hurts. I grow wise
in silent ways which speech absolves.
I grow wise and sift the fallen petals
from the ground, and press
their unmaimed fragrance to my lips
and speak and speak and urge my days
to lengthen forward once again in the good name of light.

Before Bonnard's *The Terrace,*
Sunday Afternoon

The crazed, albino man and I who sit
In front of this Bonnard, we don't quite fit

Into this crowd today: the coiffured rich
And lovely come to play at art and bitch

About the suddenly cold and severe
Climate, who tend to yak but rarely hear

The faint percussion of the talented dead
Who inhabit these rooms, and, though now wed

To the articulate silence of the grave,
Persist in being bold enough to brave

The rehearsed conversations of the lonely
And the oblique glances of the homely

Sunday lovers of antique cultures—
Cappucino-drinkers and *artiste*-vultures

Who *ooh* and *ahh* between the track-lit walls,
Leaving tendrils of perfume among the halls,

While Bonnard's pair, among the flowers,
Wile away the crowded, frenzied hours

Between now and closing time at seven
When, once again alone in Bonnard's heaven,

Theirs will be the world as he once made it—
Without the rich, the crazed, the lonely to invade it,

Without, even, this strange albino man and I,
Stealing the heavens from the painter's pale sky.

Patience

for A. R. Ammons

The young boy on the birding trail at dusk
says it can drive you crazy,
the way the birds are so hard to spot
among the dense leaves, the way you can hear them
up there but they won't come out, the way you
have to be able to recognize their calls
to make sense of the thing, and I shake my head
to agree—yes, it's a hard life here in the woods,
so many things competing for our attention,
out there to fool us, calling out
to our senses and then disappearing.
So I walk on, over the muddied path,
until I come to a spot right near the road
where a snail rests, like a thimble left on a table.
I have nowhere important to go, so I take a seat,
in a dry place next to a ravaged stump.
Minutes go by, maybe hours, until—slow
as a watched mushroom—the snail's whole house
trembles and, by God, rises. It lowers
its muscular foot into the mud and starts to crawl,
in smaller and smaller increments, to the other side.
By then, the sun has begun setting. Hours
may have passed, I don't know. But I've had
nothing to lose. I am merely a man,
in mid-age, who's been out looking for birds,
a man trying to learn something about patience—
the interdisciplinary virtue,
the one so much like love is.

The Beautiful Is the Familiar

So say that your downstairs neighbor screams in her sleep,
Alphonse, or that the drainpipe leaks, or that the putt-putt
of the radiators has kept you awake now for weeks, say
that the view from your window is not sublime, that
wherever you park your car is always declared
the alternate side of the street, or that the trash's
piled in the alley so high it resembles a monument,
or that the heat's off, and the block's just been zoned
for a golf course, say your whole life at times
is merely a razzmatazz of inappropriate things
in an inappropriate place, nonetheless it's yours
and it is January and you have just come in from the cold
to the sight of familiar cups in familiar cupboards
and the feel of your head against the sheets
is a familiar feel and the radiator hiss
like that old patient you have come to love
in the contagious hospital that is your life,
and your downstairs neighbor screams as if
there's no tomorrow, though it is merely
afternoon and you have fallen to your knees
with that bizarre, old gratitude that grips you
at peculiar times when the only thing to celebrate
is what you own and what you own and what you are
are nearly the same, though it may be you live
in a king's dominion by yourself and everything
you hallelujah for would not suffice for praise
at times like this in any other life
but does in yours, goddamn, it does it does,
and all your hallelujahs in the air for just
its plain and unromantic and for its perfect sake.

The Pleasures of Old Age

When my grandmother Lisette turned ninety-nine,
all she could think of was men—
how they would enter her room during the night
from the vast mixer of the mind, wild
with desire, drunk with a desperate love
for only her. All day she sat, spectacle-less,
over romance magazines, until, at night,
she could dream them back into her arms,
those beautiful men, and, when morning came,
rise from her immaculate bed, pink
with the glow of the newly deflowered,
to enter the world again. All over our island
that was Manhattan, bachelors sprouted like dandelions
in the field of her hungers—Baruch Oestrich, stifled
by shyness at eighty-eight, for whom she would primp for hours;
Hugo Marx, a youthful seventy-seven, but too tired to notice;
Walter Hass, a sprightly eighty, who had sat *shivah*
for his wife for thirty years. Afternoons,
like a young girl dateless at prom time,
she would wait by the phone, sure that deliverance
would come in the voice of some stranger, resolved
that her double digitry would grow centuried
in a whirl of romance. I don't know what she was thinking
that day, when she fell from the top of the stairs
to die at the bottom, but I like to imagine
it was of who would enter her room that night,
and of her great joy in beautiful men—
how she had trembled for them once,
how she would gladly tremble for them again,
even now.

Doubled

It may be that it is not, in fact, Billie Holiday
floating into the bedroom from the living room speakers,
and it may be that we are not the beautiful horses
we seem like in this long mirror beside the bed,
riding each other with the grace of skaters
in the soft lumens the flame wafts over us,
seeming so perfect here, as if pleasure itself
were a kind of artistry, as if the soft cries flesh thrusts
into the late-light were a litany, a prayer
only the infidels have access to but which grants
its good grace to the body's singleness. Yes, it may be
that this is not love at all, though it seems—
in the warmth that soothes all weather into
a single season—almost a likelihood, it may be
that all these things are true or untrue, possible
or impossible, but we are nonetheless rich, love,
in the illusion of perfection light casts on us
as I crane my neck to scan this double-pleasure
of ours, pretzeled together in the mock-fusions
love lends the lucky some nights, in the thrusts
and counterthrusts bodies speak when speech has said
all it is capable of and two people have found,
once more, the peace of their animal selves,
crying out whatever sounds first come to them,
viewing themselves, at last, as their own masterpiece,
fucking their way ever-so-gently toward sleep
as the flame flickers from above the bookcase
and some voice, I know not whose, wafts jazz
into the slow dance of what they see and what they are
as if the two were merely frames of a single vision,
as if Billie Holliday were singing just for them.

Halved

for Seamus Heaney

Last night the half moon rose over the Charles
and I thought again how we too are halved
by our losses time and time again until we
seem hardly to exist: how our parents, too,
wane from us in halves—first one, then
the other—until we ourselves are merely
a half-step from our final sleep, half feared,
half welcomed, perhaps, as a reprieve from
our own diminishments. But this night it rose,
that luminous moon, high over the half-shell
of the boathouse, like a promise half delivered,
like the small, delicate pastry of my childhood
we called a black-and-white, as if we knew
the nature of our lives, as if all we hungered for
had been seen as a half darkness. It was merely
a sliced disc of light, that moon, against a vast
carpet of emptiness, untroubled by stars.
And as I walked across the river, toward
the ghostly half-bowl of the empty stadium,
the sycamores rose like wishbones into the air,
and I thought of your mother, entirely gone,
and was glad we survive in parts to name
what we have lost, that the same moon will hang
in a half-night over your Irish house, so glad
penultimate things survive to name the night.

Dusk: Mallards
on the Charles River

So much like an old couple on their nightly walk
that they must, in fact, be one, they come now,

Webbing their way shoreward in the late light,
against the burnt sienna of the fading boathouses,

As in the dream of tranquility we all dream,
as if akin to the small solace words bring

To a man sitting alone, at dusk, on a park bench.
And they are wishless against the soft ripplings

Of the passing boats, they simply are what they are
(hardly sexed in the afterglow of the backlit sky,

Tandemed to strokes that must have preceded desire).
It is their lacks that we envy them for: speech,

Torpor, boredom and blind lust. It is the silence
of their passing this warm night that brings us

Again to what we might have become in this life
if not human—this and the doused sun dipping now

Like a bronzed wafer into the communion of evening.
And the bass urging their circles of water outward

Toward the petulant lovers. And the darkening walls:
night-struck and covered with ivy all in vain.

The End

Because he did not wish to live forever
with a sign marked *Loneliness* hung over his door,
because he did not wish to savage the light
of a deeply human love for the brief flame
of an empty posterity, because he no longer wanted
to turn each morning for the remainder of his days
and find only air beside him in the heart of the bed,
because he knew art was merely another currency
in the vast dominion of a decent life, because
he was still young enough to view change
as the best part of a steadfast spirit,
he decided to turn, now,
away from his earlier obsessions,
he decided to walk out into the day, bereft
of the other-worldly ambitions of the next life,
bereft of the empty gaze of anonymous admirers
and to put aside, for a while, the blank page
and the ubiquity of longing, he decided to live,
now, in a small empire of attainable wishes,
to take back his living blood from the cold inkwell
of a calloused heart, to forsake the sweet ease
of habitual pathos and walk out, umbrellaless,
into the rain of the tangible life. So he gazed,
now, a last time at the cool whiteness
of the blank page, he stared up
at the synergistic ease of the planets,
the bright light of some already extinguished star.
Midway toward being a spent light himself,
a terrible simplicity came over him at last
and he longed, now, for a new orbit of tethered motion,
the solace of a quieted voice not entirely his own.

He looked out at the clear hills beckoning to him.
He folded the page down the middle of his life.
He wrote the words: *THE END*.

And it was the end.

Author's Note

The author wishes to thank the Literature Program of the National Endowment for the Arts, the Ingram-Merrill Foundation, and the St. Botolph Club Foundation, without whose generous support and expressions of confidence this book would not have been possible. Also my deepest gratitude to the MacDowell Colony, for providing the time and tranquility during which some of the poems in this collection were written and revised.

It would be an act of profound ingratitude were I not to mention several friends and colleagues whose inspiration and support—personal and intellectual—has been a source of strength to me. At the risk of omitting others who deserve mention, I will name at least these: Helen Vendler, for having the generosity to believe in me more than I believe in myself; Seamus Heaney, for the intelligence, dignity and generosity of his example; Monroe and Brenda Engel, for their warmth, intelligence and human kindness; Bonnie Costello and Gail Finney, for teaching me some of what I have missed of the sisterly.

Several friends were of great help to me in their generous and sympathetic reading of this book in manuscript form. For that—and for what they have taught me not only about poetry, but about generosity—I wish to thank Lorrie Moore, Michael Collier, Gray Jacobik, Robert Gilson, Glen Hartley and Lisa Kaufman.

The author wishes to thank the following magazines and periodicals, in which some of the poems in this collection originally appeared:

The American Scholar: "Lucky"; *The American Voice:* "A Man Grieves Always for the Ships He Has Missed," "The Heart of Quang Duc"; *Antaeus:* "Dusk: Mallards on the Charles River"; *The Bennington Review:* "Before Bonnard's 'The Terrace' " (as "Before Bonnard's 'The Terrace,' Sunday Afternoon"); *Embers:* "Museum Piece," "Separated," "Skototropic"; *Kayak:* "Stones in Love"; *Michigan Quarterly Review:* "Seven O'Clock Muse"; *Mosaic:* "Patience"; *The Nation:* "Halved," "The Word 'Love,' " "The Scullers"; *The New Criterion:* "Winter Solstice, 1983"; *The New Republic:* "Garments"; *Nimrod:* "The Dangers of Metaphor"; *Oxford Poetry:* "For/ Against"; *Poetry:* "Advice to My Students: How to Write a Poem"; *Sequoia:* "Dr. Wuschti," "The Tip of the Iceberg"; *Southern Poetry Review:* "The Artichokes of Midnight"; *The Texas Review:* "At Lucy Vincent Beach," "It Happens," "Stamps"; and *Verse:* "The Pleasures of Abstraction."

"Grace" and "The Mountains of Evening" are reprinted from *Prairie Schooner* by permission of University of Nebraska Press. Copyright 1984 University of Nebraska Press.

Grateful acknowledgment is made for permission to reprint excerpts from the following copyrighted material:

"Sailing After Lunch," "The Poems of Our Climate," and "The Comedian as the Letter 'C' " from *The Collected Poems of Wallace Stevens.* Copyright 1923, renewed 1951 by Wallace Stevens. Reprinted by permission of Alfred A. Knopf, Inc., and Faber and Faber Ltd.

"The Table" from *The Complete Poems* by Carlos Drummond de Andrade, translated by Elizabeth Bishop. Copyright © 1983 by Alice Helen Methfessel. Copyright © 1969 by Elizabeth Bishop. Renewal copyright © 1980 by Alice Helen Methfessel. Reprinted by permission of Farrar, Straus & Giroux, Inc.

The Moviegoer by Walker Percy. Copyright © 1960, 1961 by Walker Percy. By permission of Alfred A. Knopf, Inc.

The Unbearable Lightness of Being: A Novel by Milan Kundera, translated from the Czech by Michael Henry Heim. English translation copyright

MICHAEL BLUMENTHAL is the author, most recently, of the memoir *All My Mothers and Fathers* (Harper Collins, 2002) and of *Dusty Angel* (BOA Editions, 1999), his sixth book of poems. His novel *Weinstock Among the Dying,* which won Hadassah Magazine's Harold U. Ribelow Prize for the best work of Jewish fiction, was published in 1994, and his collection of essays from Central Europe, *When History Enters the House,* in 1998. His collection of poems *Days We Would Rather Know* was reprinted by Pleasure Boat Studio: A Literary Press in 2005.

Speak to the Mountain is the first book published by *Aequitas Books,* an imprint of **Pleasure Boat Studio: A Literary Press**

Other books by *Pleasure Boat Studio: A Literary Press:*

Artrage * Everett Aison
ISBN 1-929355-25-4 * 225 pages * fiction * $15
Days We Would Rather Know * Michael Blumenthal
ISBN 1-929355-24-6 * 118 pages * poetry * $14
Puget Sound: 15 Stories * C. C. Long
ISBN 1-929355-22-X * 150 pages * fiction * $14
Homicide My Own * Anne Argula
ISBN 1-929355-21-1 * 220 pages * fiction (mystery) * $16
Craving Water * Mary Lou Sanelli
ISBN 1-929355-19-X * 121 pages * poetry * $15
When the Tiger Weeps * Mike O'Connor
ISBN 1-929355-18-9 * 168 pages * poetry and prose * 15
Wagner, Descending: The Wrath of the Salmon Queen * Irving Warner
ISBN 1-929355-17-3 * 242 pages * fiction * $16
Concentricity * Sheila E. Murphy
ISBN 1-929355-16-5 * 82 pages * poetry * $13.95
Schilling, from a study in lost time * Terrell Guillory
ISBN 1-929355-09-2 * 156 pages * fiction * $16.95
Rumours: A Memoir of a British POW in WWII * Chas Mayhead
ISBN 1-929355-06-8 * 201 pages * nonfiction * $16
The Immigrant's Table * Mary Lou Sanelli
ISBN 1-929355-15-7 * $13.95 * poetry and recipes * $13/95
The Enduring Vision of Norman Mailer * Dr. Barry H. Leeds
ISBN 1-929355-11-4 * criticism * $18
Women in the Garden * Mary Lou Sanelli
ISBN 1-929355-14-9 * poetry * $13.95
Pronoun Music * Richard Cohen
ISBN 1-929355-03-3 * short stories * $16
If You Were With Me Everything Would Be All Right * Ken Harvey
ISBN 1-929355-02-5 * short stories * $16
The 8th Day of the Week * Al Kessler
ISBN 1-929355-00-9 * fiction * $16
Another Life, and Other Stories * Edwin Weihe
ISBN 1-929355-011-7 * short stories * $16
Saying the Necessary * Edward Harkness
ISBN 0-9651413-7-3 (hard) $22; 0-9651413-9-X (paper) * poetry * $14
Nature Lovers * Charles Potts
ISBN 1-929355-04-1 * poetry * $10
In Memory of Hawks, & Other Stories from Alaska * Irving Warner
ISBN 0-9651413-4-9 * 210 pages * fiction * $15

The Politics of My Heart * William Slaughter
ISBN 0-9651413-0-6 * 96 pages * poetry * $12.95
The Rape Poems * Frances Driscoll
ISBN 0-9651413-1-4 * 88 pages * poetry * $12.95
When History Enters the House: Essays from Central Europe * Michael
Blumenthal
ISBN 0-9651413-2-2 * 248 pages * nonfiction * $15
Setting Out: The Education of Li-li * Tung Nien * Translated Chinese
by Mike O'Connor
ISBN 0-9651413-3-0 * 160 pages * fiction * $15

Our Chapbook Series:

No. 1: The Handful of Seeds: Three and a Half Essays * Andrew Schelling
ISBN 0-9651413-5-7 * $7 * 36 pages * nonfiction
No. 2: Original Sin * Michael Daley
ISBN 0-9651413-6-5 * $8 * 36 pages * poetry
No. 3: Too Small to Hold You * Kate Reavey
ISBN 1-92935-05-x * $8 * poetry
No. 4: The Light on Our Faces: A Therapy Dialogue *
    Lee Miriam Whitman-Raymond
ISBN 1-929355-12-2 * $8 * 36 pages * poetry
No. 5: Selected New Poems of Rainer Maria Rilke *
    Translated by Alice Derry
ISBN 1-929355-10-6 * $10 * poetry
No. 6: Through High Still Air: A Season at Sourdough Mountain *
    Tim McNulty
ISBN 1-929355-27-0 * $9 * poetry and prose
No. 7: Sight Progress * Zhang Er, Translated by Rachel Levitsky
ISBN 1-929355-28-9

From our backlist (in limited editions):

Desire * Jody Aliesan
ISBN 0-912887-11-7 * $14 * poetry (an Empty Bowl book)
Dreams of the Hand * Susan Goldwitz
ISBN 0-912887-12-5 * $14 * poetry (an Empty Bowl book)
Lineage * Mary Lou Sanelli
No ISBN * $14 * poetry (an Empty Bowl book)
The Basin: Poems from a Chinese Province * Mike O'Connor
ISBN 0-912887 - 20-6 * $10 / $20 * poetry (paper/ hardbound)
    (an Empty Bowl book)
The Straits * Michael Daley
ISBN 0-912887-04-4 * $10 * poetry (an Empty Bowl book)

In Our Hearts and Minds: The Northwest and Central America *
    Ed. Michael Daley
ISBN 0-912887-18-4 * $12 * poetry and prose (an Empty Bowl book)
The Rainshadow * Mike O'Connor
No ISBN * $16 * poetry (an Empty Bowl book)
Untold Stories * William Slaughter
ISBN 1-912887 24-9 * $10 / $20 * poetry (paper / hardbound)
    (an Empty Bowl book)
In Blue Mountain Dusk * Tim McNulty
ISBN 0-9651413-8-1 * $12.95 * poetry (a Broken Moon book)

Orders: *Pleasure Boat Studio* books are available directly from PBS
or through the following:
SPD (Small Press Distribution) Tel. 800-869-7553, Fax 510-524-0852
Partners/West Tel. 425-227-8486, Fax 425-204-2448
Baker & Taylor 800-775-1100, Fax 800-775-7480
Ingram Tel 615-793-5000, Fax 615-287-5429

Pleasure Boat Studio: A Literary Press
201 West 89th Street
New York, NY 10024
Tel: 212-362-8563 / Fax: 888-810-5308
www.pleasureboatstudio.com / pleasboat@nyc.rr.com

HOW WE GOT OUR NAME... from *Pleasure Boat Studio,* an essay written by Ouyang Xiu, Song Dynasty poet, essayist, and scholar, on the twelfth day of the twelfth month in the renwu year (January 25, 1043):

"I have heard of men of antiquity who fled from the world to distant rivers and lakes and refused to their dying day to return. They must have found some source of pleasure there. If one is not anxious for profit, even at the risk of danger, or is not convicted of a crime and forced to embark; rather, if one has a favorable breeze and gentle seas and is able to rest comfortably on a pillow and mat, sailing several hundred miles in a single day, then is boat travel not enjoyable? Of course, I have no time for such diversions. But since 'pleasure boat' is the designation of boats used for such pastimes, I have now adopted it as the name of my studio. Is there anything wrong with that?"

Translated by Ronald Egan